Plant Based Diabetic Cookbook for Beginners

1001-Day Healthy and Delicious Recipes For Beginners to Make Easy and Quick Meals.

⬤ **Pulitzer Nadiera**

Table of Contents

INTRODUCTION

According to the International Diabetes Federation, up to 463 million adults worldwide live with diabetes.

This figure is predicted to increase to up to 700 million in 2045.

The World Health Organization reports that diabetes remains a major cause of stroke, kidney failure, heart attack and blindness.

In 2019, this condition is ranked as the ninth leading cause of mortality, claiming the lives of 1.5 million people each year.

But despite these worrisome facts and figures, one thing remains true: diabetes is a condition that you can live with and manage.

And one of the most important measures for diabetes management is a healthy and proper diet.

In this book, you will learn all about this condition, and how a proper plant-based diet can help you manage it the right way.

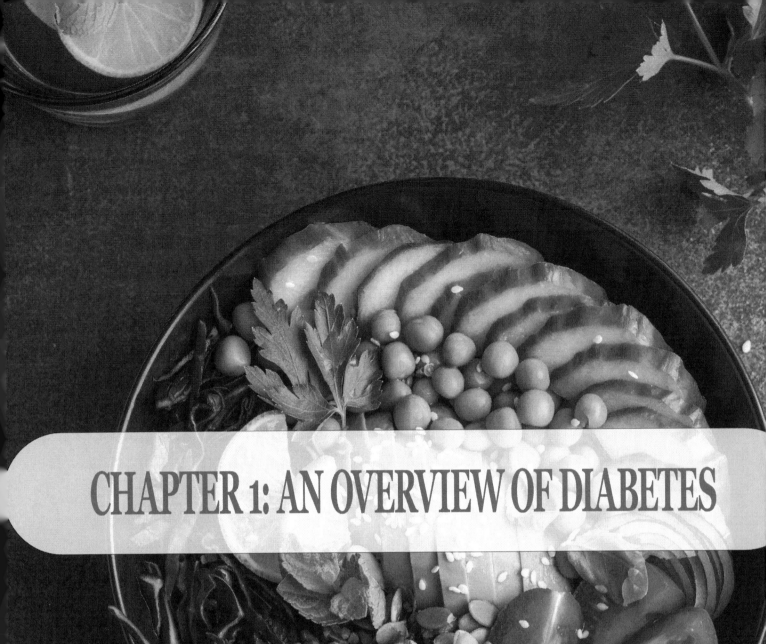

CHAPTER 1: AN OVERVIEW OF DIABETES

What is Diabetes?

Diabetes refers to a metabolic disease that causes people's blood sugar levels to spike to abnormal levels.

Insulin is a hormone inside the body that transports the sugar from the blood to the cells either for storage or for energy consumption.

When you have a condition like diabetes, the body is unable to produce sufficient insulin to carry out this task properly, or that it is unable to make proper use of the insulin that it produces.

When blood sugar levels remain at abnormal levels, this can result in damage of kidneys, eyes, nerves and other bodily organs.

Here are the different types of diabetes:

- Type 1 diabetes – This is an autoimmune disease that destroys pancreatic cells that make insulin.

- Type 2 diabetes – This is a condition in which the body resists insulin.

- Gestational diabetes – This is high blood sugar levels that occur only during pregnancy.

No matter what type of diabetes you have, a healthy and proper diet can certainly help in managing the condition.

What are the Signs and Symptoms?

Here are the general signs and symptoms of diabetes:

- Increased thirst

- Increased hunger

- Unexplained weight lossw

- Frequent urination

- Extreme fatigue

- Blurry vision

- Sores that do not heal over time

Symptoms in men

Aside from the general symptoms, men diagnosed with diabetes may also experience poor muscle strength, reduced sexual desire and erectile dysfunction.

Symptoms in women

Women on the other can also experience dry and itchy skin, yeast infections and urinary tract infections.

What are the Causes?

Diabetes is known to have a variety of causes, although some types do not clear causes.

Type 1 diabetes

For this autoimmune disease, the cause remains unclear. The immune system makes the mistake of attacking healthy cells in the pancreas and hampers the production of insulin. As to why this happens or what specific factor triggers this event, experts do not have an answer yet.

Type 2 diabetes

Genetics and lifestyle factors are pointed out as the cause of this type of diabetes. Excess weight is another possible culprit, as this makes the cells resistant to insulin effects to the blood sugar levels.

Gestational diabetes

The cause of gestational diabetes is the changes in the hormones that typically occurs during pregnancy. It is also more likely for women who are overweight or who gained too much weight during the pregnancy to suffer from this particular condition.

Diabetes Treatment and Management

Diabetes can be treated with medications and can be managed through lifestyle changes.

Type 1 diabetes

Insulin is the primary mode of treatment for this type of diabetes. The objective is to replace the insulin that the body is not able to produce. There are various types of insulin used as treatment for type 1 diabetes and these include: rapid acting insulin, short acting insulin, intermediate acting insulin and long acting insulin.

Type 2 diabetes

For people with type 2 diabetes, doctors highly recommend exercise and proper diet. If these lifestyle changes are not able to lower the levels of blood sugar, the doctor will prescribe medications.

Gestational diabetes

Proper diet and exercise ideal for pregnant women are advised for those with this condition. If these do not work, doctors will prescribe another treatment with the use of medications.

CHAPTER 2: PLANT BASED DIET FOR DIABETES MANAGEMENT

Proper Diet for Diabetes Control

Experts agree that a healthy and well-balanced diet is one of the most important facets of diabetes management.

In fact, there are some cases where in changing the diet is enough to reduce the blood sugar levels and control the condition.

Type 1 diabetes

If you have type 1 diabetes, your blood sugar levels can rise or fall depending on the food that you eat. If you eat starchy and sugary foods, your blood sugar levels tend to increase dramatically. Fat and protein, meanwhile, can increase your blood sugar levels as well, but in a more gradual manner.

Your doctor will most likely recommend you to reduce the amount of carbohydrates that you consume daily. Your carb intake would be balanced with the doses of insulin that you will take.

You can consult with a professional dietician to formulate for you a diet that has the right balance of fat, carbs and protein. This will help you manage your diabetes properly.

Type 2 diabetes

The right diet can also play in the role of treating type 2 diabetes. The right types of food will not only help reduce the blood sugar levels but can also help drop excess pounds that in turn contribute to the condition.

For people diagnosed with type 2 diabetes, it is important to count the carbs that you take in each day. This can be done with the help of a professional dietitian.

It's also essential to have small frequent meals instead of big occasional meals during the day.

Gestational diabetes

A healthy and well-balanced diet is important not only for a pregnant women with gestational diabetes but also for her baby.

It's best to limit portion sizes, reduce intake of salty and sugary foods and so on.

Consider consulting a professional dietitian to be able to formulate the right type of diet for you.

Here are some of the healthy foods that any person with any type of diabetes should eat more often:

- Fruits
- Vegetables
- Whole grains
- Lean protein sources such as fish, chicken
- Healthy fats such as nuts, olive oil

Plant Based Diet for Diabetes

What is a plant-based diet? Is it ideal for people with diabetes? These are some of the questions that some people who are diagnosed with diabetes would probably ask when recommended with the plant-based diet.

First, what is a plant-based diet? A plant-based diet is a type of diet program in which you consume foods that come mostly from plants or have little to no ingredients coming from animal food sources.

A plant-based diet is focused primarily on fruits, vegetables, whole grains, nuts, seeds and legumes.

Benefits of a Plant-Based Diet for Diabetes

Changes in one's diet and lifestyle can definitely do wonders in treating your diabetes. And switching to a plant-based diet can help you achieve the following benefits:

- Reduce risk of type 2 diabetes – If you are in the pre-diabetes stage for now, switching to a plant-based diet can greatly help reduce your risk to developing type 2 diabetes. Studies have shown that people who eat a plant-based diet are at much lower risk of developing type 2 diabetes than people who maintain a diet that's heavy on meat and animal food products.

- Lower blood sugar levels – Now if you have already been diagnosed with type 1 or type 2 diabetes, a plant-based diet can help maintain proper levels of blood sugar. Research has proven that a low-fat plant-based diet can significantly improve blood lipids and glycemic control.

- Lower body weight – As mentioned earlier, excess weight can be contributory to the onset or worsening of diabetes. When you eat a plant-based diet, the tendency is for you to lose weight. And this in turn can also help you manage this condition. Not only that, when you lose weight, you also lower the risk of other conditions like heart disease, stroke and hypertension.

- Increased intake of fiber – Since plant-based diets are rich in fiber, you will benefit from this as fiber can help slow down sugar absorption, and therefore, prevent abnormal or abrupt spikes in the blood sugar levels.

Guidelines and Tips for a Plant Based Diet for Diabetics

It's true that there are countless health benefits that you can get from eating a plant-based diet if you have been diagnosed with diabetes.

However, you need to make sure that you are getting all the essential nutrients that you need.

Nutrients such as iron, protein, B vitamins, vitamin D, iron and calcium have been found to be deficient in some of the people who maintain a plant-based diet.

The good news is, there are many plant-based food sources that can provide these nutrients.

Protein for example can be provided by legumes such as lentils, peas and beans, as well as by nuts and seeds. It would also be helpful to take in dietary supplements to make sure that you are getting all the essential nutrients that your body needs to stay in top shade.

Vitamin B12 for example cannot be obtained from any plant source. This is why, vitamin B12 deficiency is very common among people who maintain a plant-based diet. But this vitamin is needed by the body for a myriad of important processes as well as for maintain stable levels of blood sugar.

For this reason, it would be best to take in a supplement for this vitamin. You will also benefit from eating milks and cereals that are fortified with vitamin B12. Experts recommend 4 micrograms of vitamin B12 a day and 4.5 micrograms if you are pregnant.

It would also be a good idea to consult a professional dietitian to ensure that you are getting the right amount of nutrients.

Here are some more tips to help you maintain a healthy plant-based diet if you have diabetes:

- Eat foods that are high in phytochemicals and antioxidants such as berries, beans, nuts, seeds and green leafy vegetables.

- Monitor your blood sugar levels before and after mealtime so you can see the effect of your plant-based diet on your blood sugar.

- Make sure to inform your doctor if you are going to switch to a plant-based diet before starting with it. It's possible that your doctor will adjust your insulin or medication according to your dietary changes.

- Monitor the carbohydrate content of plant-based foods. You have to remember that plant-based protein foods usually have more carbohydrates than animal-based protein foods.

- Keep a logbook of your diet. Record the foods that you take as well as your blood sugar levels after each meal.

Common Concerns

Careful planning is imperative when switching to a plant-based diet. As mentioned earlier, not all nutrients can be found in plant-based food sources.

With proper planning, you will be able to get right amounts of fat, protein, carbohydrates, vitamins and minerals that you need to stay in top shape.

Always keep in mind that when you have diabetes, lowering your blood sugar level is not your only concern. You should not forget about your overall health of course.

If there is any issue that arises while you're in a plant-based diet, then be sure to inform your doctor right away.

Do not switch to this diet with consulting your doctor first as there might be a need to adjust your medications.

CHAPTER 3: BREAKFAST RECIPES

Cinnamon Oats

Preparation Time: 8 hours and 5 minutes
Cooking Time: 0 minutes
Servings: 5

Ingredients:

- 2 ½ cups rolled oats
- 2 ½ cups milk
- 8 teaspoons brown sugar
- 1 ¼ teaspoons ground cinnamon
- 2 ½ teaspoons vanilla extract
- Pinch salt

Method:

1. Combine all the ingredients in a bowl.
2. Divide mixture among 5 glass jars.
3. Seal the jar.
4. Refrigerate for 8 hours.

Serving Suggestions: Serve with fresh fruits.

Preparation & Cooking Tips: This can be refrigerated for up to 5 days.

Nutritions Value (Amount per Serving):

- Calories: 224
- Fat: 7.3
- Carbs: 44.81
- Protein: 12

Blueberry & Almond Pudding

Preparation Time: 8 hours and 10 minutes
Cooking Time: 0 minutes
Servings: 1

Ingredients:

- ½ cup milk
- 2 teaspoons maple syrup
- ⅛ teaspoon almond extract
- 2 tablespoons chia seeds
- 1 tablespoon almonds, toasted and slivered
- ½ cup fresh blueberries

Method:

1. In a bowl, mix the milk, maple syrup, almond extract and chia seeds.
2. Cover and refrigerate for 8 hours.
3. Top with almonds and blueberries.

Serving Suggestions: Stir well before serving.

Preparation & Cooking Tips: Milk mixture can be refrigerated for up to 3 days.

Nutritions Value (Amount per Serving):

- Calories: 229
- Fat: 5.12
- Carbs: 43.15
- Protein: 4.98

Oatmeal

Preparation Time: 15 minutes
Cooking Time: 10 minutes
Servings: 1

Ingredients:

- 1 cup milk
- Pinch of salt
- ½ cup rolled oats
- 1 teaspoon honey
- Pinch cinnamon powder

Method:

1. Add milk and salt to a pot over medium heat.
2. Bring to a boil.
3. Stir in the rolled oats.
4. Reduce heat and simmer for 5 minutes.
5. Turn off heat.
6. Let cool for 2 minutes.
7. Stir in honey and cinnamon before serving.

Serving Suggestions: Top with nuts or dried fruit.

Preparation & Cooking Tips: Use oats labeled as gluten free.

Nutritions Value (Amount per Serving):

- Calories: 292
- Fat: 11.32
- Carbs: 50.73
- Protein: 15.94

Avocado Toast with Tuna

Preparation Time: 5 minutes
Cooking Time: 0 minutes
Servings: 2

Ingredients:

- ¼ avocado, peeled, pitted and mashed
- 1 slice rye bread, toasted
- 1 tablespoon canned tuna flakes

Method:

1. Spread the mashed avocado on top of the rye bread.
2. Top with the tuna flakes.

Serving Suggestions: Garnish with chopped parsley.

Preparation & Cooking Tips: You can also use any type of whole-grain bread.

Nutritions Value (Amount per Serving):

- Calories: 111
- Fat: 4.48
- Carbs: 2.15
- Protein: 16.54

Peanut Butter Toast with Banana

Preparation Time: 5 minutes
Cooking Time: 0 minutes
Servings: 1

Ingredients:

- 1 tablespoon natural peanut butter
- 1 slice whole wheat bread, toasted
- 1 banana, sliced
- Pinch cinnamon powder

Method:

1. Spread peanut butter on top of the bread.
2. Top with the banana slices.
3. Sprinkle with cinnamon.

Serving Suggestions: Serve with unsweetened coffee.

Preparation & Cooking Tips: Use ripe bananas.

Nutritions Value (Amount per Serving):

- Calories: 521
- Fat: 8.69
- Carbs: 112.19
- Protein: 11.4

Berry Breakfast Smoothie

Preparation Time: 5 minutes
Cooking Time: 0 minutes
Servings: 2

Ingredients:

- 1 pear, peeled and diced
- 1 apple, peeled and diced
- 1 cup strawberries, sliced
- ½ cup raspberries, sliced
- ½ cup blueberries, sliced
- 1 cup water
- 1 cup yogurt

Method:

1. Combine all the ingredients in a blender.
2. Process until smooth.
3. Chill before serving.

Serving Suggestions: Refrigerate for 30 minutes before serving.

Preparation & Cooking Tips: You can also use frozen berries for this recipe.

Nutritions Value (Amount per Serving):

- Calories: 285
- Fat: 4.78
- Carbs: 59.37
- Protein: 6.22

Breakfast Bowl

Preparation Time: 10 minutes
Cooking Time: 10 minutes
Servings: 2

Ingredients:

- 1 ¾ cups almond milk (unsweetened)
- 1 cup rolled oats
- 2 tablespoons hemp seeds
- ¼ cup chia seeds
- ½ teaspoon ginger, grated
- Salt to taste
- 1 tablespoon maple syrup
- 2 tablespoons tahini
- ½ cup pistachios
- ½ grapefruit, sliced

Method:

1. Pour almond milk into a pot over medium heat.
2. Stir in oats and seeds.
3. Bring to a boil.
4. Reduce heat.
5. Add ginger and season with salt.
6. Simmer for 5 minutes.
7. Turn off heat.
8. Stir in maple syrup and tahini.
9. Top with pistachios and grapefruit.

Serving Suggestions: Serve with additional almond milk.

Preparation & Cooking Tips: Use roasted pistachios if available.

Nutritions Value (Amount per Serving):

- Calories: 836
- Fat: 49.89
- Carbs: 94.88
- Protein: 29.45

Blueberry Cereal

Preparation Time: 20 minutes
Cooking Time: 30 minutes
Servings: 2

Ingredients:

- 1 ½ cups blueberries
- 3 cups oat flour
- 1 cup date paste

Method:

1. Puree blueberries in a blender.
2. Mix the pureed blueberries, oat flour and date paste.
3. Form balls from the mixture.
4. Place the balls in a baking pan.
5. Bake in the oven at 375 degrees F for 30 minutes.

Serving Suggestions: Let cool for 2 hours.

Preparation & Cooking Tips: You can also use other berries for this recipe.

Nutritions Value (Amount per Serving):

- Calories: 1006
- Fat: 15.15
- Carbs: 199.99
- Protein: 25.92

Berry, Almond & Coconut Smoothie Bowl

Preparation Time: 15 minutes
Cooking Time: 0 minutes
Servings: 4

Ingredients:

- ½ cup almond milk (unsweetened)
- ½ cup banana, sliced
- ⅔ cup raspberries
- 5 tablespoons almonds, sliced
- ⅛ teaspoon ground cardamom
- ¼ teaspoon ground cinnamon
- ⅛ teaspoon vanilla extract
- 1 tablespoon coconut flakes
- ¼ cup blueberries

Method:

1. Add all the ingredients except coconut flakes and blueberries in a blender.
2. Process until pureed.
3. Transfer to serving bowls.
4. Sprinkle the coconut flakes on top.
5. Serve with the blueberries.

Serving Suggestions: Serve with additional almond milk.

Nutritions Value (Amount per Serving):

- Calories: 127
- Fat: 1.83
- Carbs: 28.61
- Protein: 1.51

Oatmeal with Chia & Quinoa

Preparation Time: 10 minutes
Cooking Time: 10 minutes
Servings: 12

Ingredients:

- 2 cups rolled oats
- 1 teaspoon ground cinnamon
- 1 cup barley flakes
- ½ cup chia seeds
- 1 cup quinoa
- Pinch salt
- 1 cup almond milk

Method:

1. Combine all the ingredients except almond milk in a bowl.
2. Pour the milk into a pot over medium heat.
3. Bring to a boil.
4. Stir in the mixture.
5. Simmer for 5 minutes.

Serving Suggestions: Serve with dried fruits.

Preparation & Cooking Tips: You can also use hemp seeds in place of chia seeds.

Nutritions Value (Amount per Serving):

- Calories: 252
- Fat: 8.22
- Carbs: 42.43
- Protein: 9.62

CHAPTER 4: LUNCH & DINNER RECIPES

Chickpea Curry

Preparation Time: 15 minutes
Cooking Time: 15 minutes
Servings: 6

Ingredients:

- 1 onion, chopped
- 4 cloves garlic
- 1 tablespoon ginger, chopped
- 1 serrano pepper, sliced
- 6 tablespoons vegetable oil
- 2 teaspoons ground cumin
- ½ teaspoon ground turmeric
- 2 teaspoons ground coriander
- 2 ¼ cups unsalted canned tomatoes
- 30 oz. canned chickpeas, rinsed and drained
- 2 teaspoons garam masala

Method:

1. Add onion, garlic, ginger and pepper to a food processor.
2. Pulse until minced.
3. Add the oil to a pan over medium heat.
4. Cook the onion mixture for 3 minutes.
5. Stir in the spices.
6. Cook for 2 minutes, stirring often.
7. Pour in the tomatoes and chickpeas.
8. Season with garam masala.
9. Simmer for 10 minutes.

Serving Suggestions: Garnish with fresh cilantro.

Nutritions Value (Amount per Serving):

- Calories: 401
- Fat: 18.15
- Carbs: 51.68
- Protein: 14.31

Vegan Buddha Bowl

Preparation Time: 15 minutes
Cooking Time: 0 minutes
Servings: 4

Ingredients:

- 4 cups quinoa, cooked
- 2 cups baby beets, cooked
- 5 oz. kale, chopped
- ½ cup hummus
- 1 avocado, sliced

Method:

1. Add the quinoa to serving bowls.
2. Top with the beets, kale and hummus.
3. Serve with the avocado slices.

Serving Suggestions: Sprinkle toasted sunflower seeds

Preparation & Cooking Tips: Add avocado only when ready to serve.

Nutritions Value (Amount per Serving):

- Calories: 815
- Fat: 20.81
- Carbs: 131.11
- Protein: 29.45

Roasted Root Vegetables

Preparation Time: 20 minutes
Cooking Time: 30 minutes
Servings: 2

Ingredients:

- 1 cup carrots, sliced
- 1 cup beets, sliced
- 1 cup turnips, sliced
- Olive oil
- 1 clove garlic, minced
- 1 teaspoon ground coriander
- ⅛ teaspoon ground pepper
- Salt and pepper to taste

Method:

1. Add the vegetables to a baking pan.
2. Drizzle with olive oil.
3. Sprinkle with minced garlic.
4. Season with the spices.
5. Roast in the oven at 375 degrees F for 30 minutes, stirring once or twice.

Serving Suggestions: Garnish with chopped parsley.

Preparation & Cooking Tips: You can also use garlic powder instead of minced garlic.

Nutritions Value (Amount per Serving):

- Calories: 241
- Fat: 14.66
- Carbs: 25.48
- Protein: 3.97

Potato Curry

Preparation Time: 15 minutes
Cooking Time: 15 minutes
Servings: 4

Ingredients:

- 3 tablespoons vegetable oil
- 1 onion, sliced
- 3 cloves garlic, minced
- 1 lb. potatoes, sliced and boiled
- 2 teaspoons curry powder
- ¼ teaspoon cayenne pepper
- Salt and pepper to taste
- 14 oz. canned tomatoes
- ¼ cup water

Method:

1. Add the oil to a pan over medium heat.
2. Cook the onion and garlic for 3 minutes, stirring often.
3. Add the potatoes.
4. Season with spices.
5. Cook while stirring for 2 minutes.
6. Pour in tomatoes and water.
7. Simmer for 10 minutes.

Serving Suggestions: Garnish with chopped parsley.

Preparation & Cooking Tips: You can also add chickpeas or green peas to the dish.

Nutritions Value (Amount per Serving):

- Calories: 204
- Fat: 10.75
- Carbs: 25.9
- Protein: 3.63

Beef & Butternut Squash Stew

Preparation Time: 15 minutes
Cooking Time: 1 hour and 30 minutes
Servings: 4

Ingredients:

- 3 tablespoon olive oil
- 1 onion, sliced
- 2 cloves garlic, minced
- 1 tablespoon fresh rosemary, minced
- 1 tablespoon fresh thyme, minced
- ½ lb. beef, sliced into cubes
- Salt and pepper to taste
- ¼ cup sun-dried tomatoes, chopped
- 4 cups beef broth
- 1 cup Marsala wine
- 1 lb. butternut squash, sliced into cubes

Method:

1. Add olive oil to a pan over medium heat.
2. Cook the onion and garlic for 2 minutes.
3. Stir in the herbs.
4. Add the beef and season with salt and pepper.
5. Cook until browned.
6. Add the rest of the ingredients.
7. Reduce heat.
8. Cook for 1 hour and 30 minutes.

Serving Suggestions: Serve with crusty bread.

Preparation & Cooking Tips: Add water and flour to thicken the sauce.

Nutritions Value (Amount per Serving):

- Calories: 322
- Carbs: 37.08
- Fat: 13.89
- Protein: 15.16

Garlic Squash

Preparation Time: 15 minutes
Cooking Time: 45 minutes
Servings: 10

Ingredients:

- 5 lb. squash, sliced into cubes
- 2 tablespoons olive oil
- Salt and pepper to taste
- 3 cloves garlic, minced

Method:

1. Preheat your oven to 375 degrees F.
2. Toss the squash cubes in olive oil.
3. Season with salt and pepper.
4. Spread squash in a baking pan.
5. Roast for 45 minutes.

Serving Suggestions: Sprinkle with parsley before serving.

Preparation & Cooking Tips: You can also use other types of winter squash for this recipe.

Nutritions Value (Amount per Serving):

- Calories: 118
- Fat: 2.94
- Carbs: 24.36
- Protein: 1.96

Lemon Roasted Cauliflower & Broccoli

Preparation Time: 20 minutes
Cooking Time: 30 minutes
Servings: 4

Ingredients:

- 2 cups cauliflower florets
- 2 cups broccoli florets
- 1 tablespoon olive oil
- 1 teaspoon lemon juice
- 2 cloves garlic, minced
- 1 teaspoon dried oregano
- Salt and pepper to taste

Method:

1. Combine all the ingredients in a baking pan.
2. Toss to coat evenly.
3. Bake in the oven at 375 degrees F for 30 minutes.

Serving Suggestions: Garnish with lemon wedges.

Preparation & Cooking Tips: You can also use lemon zest to flavor up the vegetables.

Nutritions Value (Amount per Serving):

- Calories: 55
- Fat: 3.67
- Carbs: 5.05
- Protein: 2.01

Roasted Tofu

Preparation Time: 15 minutes
Cooking Time: 1 hour
Servings: 4

Ingredients:

- ¼ cup low-sodium soy sauce
- ¼ cup lime juice
- 6 tablespoons toasted sesame oil
- 28 oz. tofu, sliced into cubes

Method:

1. Preheat your oven to 325 degrees F.
2. In a bowl, mix the soy sauce, lime juice and sesame oil.
3. Soak the tofu in the mixture for 10 minutes.
4. Spread tofu to a baking pan.
5. Bake in the oven for 1 hour or until golden and crispy.

Serving Suggestions: Garnish with lime slices.

Preparation & Cooking Tips: Lemon juice can also be used in place of lime juice.

Nutritions Value (Amount per Serving):

- Calories: 731
- Fat: 60.51
- Carbs: 22.98
- Protein: 35.62

Kale, Sweet Potato & Tofu Salad

Preparation Time: 5 minutes
Cooking Time: 0 minutes
Servings: 2

Ingredients:

- 1 sweet potato, sliced into cubes and roasted
- 2 cups kale, shredded
- 2 cups tofu, sliced into cubes and baked
- Vinaigrette

Method:

1. Mix all the ingredients in a bowl.
2. Drizzle with vinaigrette.

Serving Suggestions: Sprinkle with chopped pecans before serving.

Preparation & Cooking Tips: You can also add quinoa to this salad.

Nutritions Value (Amount per Serving):

- Calories: 263
- Fat: 5.07
- Carbs: 45.24
- Protein: 10.29

Sauteed Cauliflower

Preparation Time: 15 minutes
Cooking Time: 15 minutes
Servings: 2

Ingredients:

- 2 teaspoons olive oil
- 1 clove garlic, minced
- 2 cups cauliflower florets
- ¼ cup low-sodium chicken broth
- 3 tablespoons water
- Salt and pepper to taste

Method:

1. Pour the oil into a pan over medium heat.
2. Add garlic and cook for 30 seconds.
3. Stir in the cauliflower.
4. Cook for 10 minutes or until tender.
5. Pour in the chicken broth and water.
6. Season with salt and pepper.
7. Cover and cook for 2 minutes.

Serving Suggestions: Top with crispy garlic bits.

Nutritions Value (Amount per Serving):

- Calories: 83
- Fat: 5.03
- Carbs: 8.3
- Protein: 3.2

Mushroom & Barley Risotto

Preparation Time: 15 minutes
Cooking Time: 10 minutes
Servings: 4

Ingredients:

- 2 tablespoons olive oil
- 1 onion, chopped
- 4 cloves garlic, minced
- 3 tablespoons white wine
- 8 cups vegetable broth
- 1 ½ cups pearl barley
- 1 tablespoon lemon juice
- Salt and pepper to taste
- 4 cups mushrooms, cooked
- ¼ cup caramelized onions

Method:

1. Pour the oil to a pan over medium low heat.
2. Cook the onion and garlic for 3 minutes.
3. Pour in the white wine and vegetable broth.
4. Stir in the barley.
5. Cook until liquid has been absorbed.
6. Turn off heat.
7. Transfer to a serving plate.
8. Stir in the rest of the ingredients.

Serving Suggestions: Serve with arugula.

Nutritions Value (Amount per Serving):

- Calories: 393
- Fat: 8.03
- Carbs: 73.12
- Protein: 11.26

Sesame Beets

Preparation Time: 15 minutes
Cooking Time: 45 minutes
Servings: 4

Ingredients:

- 4 cups beets, peeled and chopped
- 3 tablespoons sesame oil
- 1 leek, chopped
- 2 cloves garlic, minced
- 1 tablespoon ginger, grated
- 2 tablespoons liquid aminos
- Salt and pepper to taste

Method:

1. Preheat your oven to 400 degrees F.
2. Spread the beets in a baking pan.
3. Drizzle with sesame oil.
4. Roast in the oven for 30 minutes, turning once.
5. Stir in the rest of the ingredients.
6. Roast for another 15 minutes.

Serving Suggestions: Sprinkle white sesame seeds on top.

Preparation & Cooking Tips: You can also use soy sauce in place of liquid aminos.

Nutritions Value (Amount per Serving):

- Calories: 276
- Fat: 12.28
- Carbs: 42.35
- Protein: 2.67

Orange & Arugula Salad

Preparation Time: 15 minutes
Cooking Time: 0 minutes
Servings: 4

Ingredients:

Salad
- 4 cups arugula
- 1 orange, sliced into segments
- ½ cup pistachios, chopped

Dressing
- 2 tablespoons apple cider vinegar
- 1 tablespoon orange juice
- 1 teaspoon soy sauce
- ¼ cup roasted pistachios
- ¼ teaspoon ginger, grated
- Salt and pepper to taste

Method:

1. Arrange arugula in a salad plate.
2. Top with orange slices and pistachios.
3. Add the dressing ingredients to a food processor or blender.
4. Process until smooth.
5. Drizzle dressing over the salad and serve.

Serving Suggestions: Garnish with fresh cilantro.

Preparation & Cooking Tips: You can also add thinly sliced fennel to the salad.

Nutritions Value (Amount per Serving):

- Calories: 179
- Fat: 10.96
- Carbs: 17
- Protein: 5.97

Superfood Salad

Preparation Time: 10 minutes
Cooking Time: 0 minutes
Servings: 8

Ingredients:

- 1 red cabbage, shredded
- 4 carrots, sliced into strips
- 1 beet, sliced thinly
- 1 avocado, peeled, pitted and sliced thinly
- 2/3 cup walnuts, chopped

Dressing

- ½ cup olive oil
- ¼ cup apple cider vinegar
- 2 cloves garlic, peeled
- Salt to taste

Method:

1. Toss the vegetables and avocado in a salad bowl.
2. Top with the walnuts.
3. Add all the dressing ingredients to a blender or food processor.
4. Serve the salad with the dressing on the side.

Serving Suggestions: Sprinkle dried basil on top of the salad before serving.

Preparation & Cooking Tips: Green cabbage can also be used for this recipe.

Nutritions Value (Amount per Serving):

- Calories: 230
- Fat: 21.61
- Carbs: 9.59
- Protein: 1.94

Tofu Stir Fry

Preparation Time: 45 minutes
Cooking Time: 20 minutes
Servings: 6

Ingredients:

- 1 block tofu, sliced into cubes
- 2 cups sesame ginger salad dressing, divided
- ¼ cup sesame oil
- 2 cups button mushrooms, sliced
- 1 cup broccoli florets
- ¼ cup almonds, toasted and slivered
- ¼ cup vegetable broth
- 1 cup corn starch
- 1 tablespoon soy sauce
- 1 teaspoon sugar substitute

Method:

1. Marinate the tofu in 1 cup sesame ginger salad dressing for 30 minutes.
2. Pour the sesame oil to a pan over medium heat.
3. Cook the tofu for 7 minutes, stirring often.
4. Stir in the mushrooms and broccoli.
5. Cook while stirring for 2 minutes.
6. Add the almonds.
7. In a bowl, mix the remaining ingredients.
8. Add the mixture to the pan.
9. Reduce heat and simmer for 10 minutes.

Serving Suggestions: Serve in lettuce cups.

Preparation & Cooking Tips: You can also omit sugar substitute in the recipe.

Nutritions Value (Amount per Serving):

- Calories: 603
- Fat: 50.71
- Carbs: 30.68
- Protein: 10.68

Black Bean Salad

Preparation Time: 10 minutes
Cooking Time: 0 minutes
Servings: 6

Ingredients:

- 2 tablespoons olive oil
- ½ cup onion, sliced thinly
- 1 clove garlic, minced
- 1 ripe avocado, pitted and chopped
- ¼ cup cilantro leaves
- ¼ cup lime juice
- Pinch salt
- 8 cups salad greens
- 1 cup tomatoes, sliced
- 15 oz. canned black beans, rinsed and drained

Method:

1. Combine oil, onion, garlic, avocado, cilantro, lime juice and salt in a blender or food processor.
2. Process until smooth.
3. Mix the salad greens, tomatoes and black beans.
4. Top with the dressing.

Serving Suggestions: Drizzle with dressing or serve dressing on the side.

Preparation & Cooking Tips: You can also top with crispy fried tofu cubes.

Nutritions Value (Amount per Serving):

- Calories: 1512
- Fat: 151.31
- Carbs: 31.99
- Protein: 7.89

Butternut Squash Carbonara

Preparation Time: 15 minutes
Cooking Time: 20 minutes
Servings: 8

Ingredients:

- 2 tablespoons olive oil
- 1 onion, chopped
- 4 cloves garlic, divided
- 1 lb. butternut squash, peeled and sliced into cubes
- ½ cup almonds, chopped
- 1 tablespoon fresh sage, chopped
- 1 cup cream
- Salt and pepper to taste
- 8 cups spaghetti, cooked

Method:

1. Add the oil to a pan over medium heat.
2. Cook onion and garlic for 2 minutes.
3. Stir in the squash.
4. Cook for 10 to 15 minutes, stirring often.
5. Add the rest of the ingredients except pasta.
6. Cook for 3 minutes.
7. Top the pasta with the sauce.

Serving Suggestions: Sprinkle with pepper before serving.

Preparation & Cooking Tips: You can also add eggs to the sauce.

Nutritions Value (Amount per Serving):

- Calories: 299
- Fat: 10.08
- Carbs: 47.36
- Protein: 9.24

Potatoes with Beans & Salsa

Preparation Time: 15 minutes
Cooking Time: 45 minutes
Servings: 4

Ingredients:

- 4 potatoes, sliced
- 1 tablespoon olive oil
- 1 cup salsa
- 2 tablespoons jalapenos, chopped
- 15 oz. pinto beans, cooked

Method:

1. Preheat your oven to 425 degrees F.
2. Toss potato slices in olive oil.
3. Roast in the oven for 45 minutes.
4. Top with the salsa, jalapenos and pinto beans.

Serving Suggestions: Serve with sour cream.

Preparation & Cooking Tips: You can also serve with nacho chips.

Nutritions Value (Amount per Serving):

- Calories: 702
- Fat: 5.31
- Carbs: 135.34
- Protein: 31.23

Chickpea & Avocado Salad

Preparation Time: 15 minutes
Cooking Time: 0 minutes
Servings: 2

Ingredients:

- 3 tablespoons olive oil
- 1 clove garlic, peeled
- 3 tablespoons lemon juice
- 2 teaspoons lemon zest
- Salt to taste
- 5 oz. mixed greens
- 1 carrot, shredded
- ½ avocado, sliced into cubes
- 1 cup chickpeas

Method:

1. Add olive oil, garlic, lemon juice, lemon zest and salt to a food processor or blender.
2. Process until smooth.
3. Top the mixed greens with carrot, avocado and chickpeas.
4. Drizzle dressing over salad and serve.

Serving Suggestions: Top with shaved cheese.

Preparation & Cooking Tips: Kale and spinach can also be used for this recipe.

Nutritions Value (Amount per Serving):

- Calories: 674
- Fat: 33.9
- Carbs: 75.66
- Protein: 23.51

Tuna Salad

Preparation Time: 45 minutes
Cooking Time: 0 minutes
Servings: 4

Ingredients:

- 5 oz. tuna flakes
- 1 red bell pepper, diced
- ½ cup red onion, chopped
- ½ cup parsley, chopped
- 2 tablespoons capers, chopped
- 4 tablespoons mayonnaise
- 1 tablespoon lemon juice
- Salt and pepper to taste

Method:

1. Combine all the ingredients in a bowl.
2. Refrigerate for 30 minutes.

Serving Suggestions: Serve on top of lettuce.

Preparation & Cooking Tips: Use canned tuna flakes packed in water.

Nutritions Value (Amount per Serving):

- Calories: 226
- Fat: 14.87
- Carbs: 22.48
- Protein: 2.95

CHAPTER 5: SOUP RECIPES

Sweet Potato Coconut Soup

Preparation Time: 15 minutes
Cooking Time: 50 minutes
Servings: 6

Ingredients:

- 2 tablespoons olive oil
- 1 ½ cups yellow onion, diced
- 1 clove garlic, minced
- 1 tablespoon ginger, minced
- 1 lb. sweet potatoes, sliced into cubes
- 3 cups water
- 1 cup coconut milk
- 4 teaspoons red curry paste
- Salt and pepper to taste

Method:

1. Add the oil to a pot over medium heat.
2. Cook onion, garlic and ginger for 3 minutes, stirring often.
3. Add sweet potatoes.
4. Cook for 15 minutes, stirring often.
5. Add the rest of the ingredients.
6. Reduce heat and simmer for 30 minutes.

Serving Suggestions: Top with roasted peanuts.

Preparation & Cooking Tips: The soup can be refrigerated for up to 3 days.

Nutritions Value (Amount per Serving):

- Calories: 192
- Fat: 16.2
- Carbs: 11.82
- Protein: 3.33

Tomato & Mushroom Soup

Preparation Time: 15 minutes
Cooking Time: 30 minutes
Servings: 6

Ingredients:

- 1 tablespoons olive oil
- 1 onion, chopped
- 3 garlic cloves, minced
- 1 leek, sliced
- 1 cup mushrooms
- ½ cup basil, chopped
- 4 cups vegetable broth
- ¼ cup tomato paste
- 5 cups canned diced tomatoes
- Salt and pepper to taste

Method:

1. Add the olive oil to a pot over medium heat.
2. Cook onion for 3 minutes.
3. Stir in the garlic and leek.
4. Cook for 2 minutes.
5. Add mushrooms and basil.
6. Cook while stirring for 5 minutes.
7. Add the rest of the ingredients.
8. Simmer for 20 minutes.

Serving Suggestions: Garnish with additional basil.

Preparation & Cooking Tips: You can also add tortellini to this soup.

Nutritions Value (Amount per Serving):

- Calories: 85
- Fat: 2.7
- Carbs: 14.51
- Protein: 2.79

Persian Squash Soup

Preparation Time: 30 minutes
Cooking Time: 45 minutes
Servings: 6

Ingredients:

- 1 butternut squash, sliced into cubes
- 3 tablespoons olive oil
- ¾ teaspoon ground cumin
- ½ teaspoon ground cinnamon
- ¼ teaspoon ground coriander
- Salt and pepper to taste
- 2 cups water

Method:

1. Toss squash cubes in olive oil.
2. Roast in the oven at 425 degrees F for 30 minutes.
3. Let cool.
4. Transfer to a blender along with the rest of the ingredients.
5. Process until pureed.
6. Transfer to a pot.
7. Heat through for 15 minutes.

Serving Suggestions: Sprinkle with ground sumac before serving.

Preparation & Cooking Tips: Add saffron thread to the soup.

Nutritions Value (Amount per Serving):

- Calories: 75
- Fat: 6.85
- Carbs: 3.73
- Protein: 0.44

Tofu Miso Soup

Preparation Time: 20 minutes
Cooking Time: 40 minutes
Servings: 6

Ingredients:

- 4 cups water
- ¼ cup scallions, sliced thinly
- 2 cloves garlic, minced
- 2 teaspoons toasted sesame oil
- ¼ cup strip steak, sliced into thin strips and cooked
- Pepper to taste
- ½ cup tofu, diced and cooked
- 2 tablespoons white miso

Method:

1. Combine all the ingredients except tofu and miso in a pot over medium heat.
2. Bring to a boil.
3. Reduce heat and simmer for 30 minutes.
4. Stir in the miso and top with the tofu.

Serving Suggestions: Top with dried seaweed.

Nutritions Value (Amount per Serving):

- Calories: 74
- Fat: 3.86
- Carbs: 6.34
- Protein: 3.65

Vegetable Soup with Chicken

Preparation Time: 15 minutes
Cooking Time: 40 minutes
Servings: 7

Ingredients:

- 1 tablespoon olive oil
- 1 onion, sliced
- 1 carrot, diced
- ¼ cup chicken breast, sliced into cubes and cooked
- 1 stalk celery, diced
- ¼ cup mushrooms, slice
- 2 cups chicken broth
- 1 teaspoon dried thyme
- 1 teaspoon dried oregano
- Salt and pepper to taste

Method:

1. Pour the olive oil to a pot over medium heat.
2. Add onion and cook for 1 minute.
3. Add carrot and cook until tender.
4. Stir in the rest of the ingredients.
5. Bring to a boil.
6. Reduce heat and simmer for 30 minutes.

Serving Suggestions: Sprinkle with pepper before serving.

Preparation & Cooking Tips: You can also use fresh herbs for this recipe.

Nutritions Value (Amount per Serving):

- Calories: 151
- Fat: 7.68
- Carbs: 2.3
- Protein: 17.24

Vegetable & Basil Soup

Preparation Time: 10 minutes
Cooking Time: 20 minutes
Servings: 4

Ingredients:

- 2 teaspoons olive oil
- 1 clove garlic, minced
- ¼ cup onion, chopped
- ¼ cup carrots, chopped
- ¼ cup cabbage, shredded
- ¼ cup basil, chopped
- 4 cups vegetable broth

Method:

1.Add olive oil to a pot over medium heat.
2.Cook the garlic and onion for 2 minutes, stirring often.
3.Stir in the carrots.
4.Cook for 5 minutes.
5.Stir in the rest of the ingredients.
6.Simmer for 10 minutes.

Serving Suggestions: Garnish with additional basil.

Nutritions Value (Amount per Serving):

- Calories: 1908
- Fat: 220.3
- Carbs: 2.03
- Protein: 0.32

Coconut & Chicken Soup

Preparation Time: 15 minutes
Cooking Time: 45 minutes
Servings: 6

Ingredients:

- ¼ cup chicken breast, sliced thinly
- Salt and pepper to taste
- 1 tablespoon coconut oil
- 1 onion, sliced
- 2 cloves garlic, minced
- 1 tablespoon ginger, grated
- 1 cup squash, sliced into cubes
- 14 oz. coconut milk
- 2 cups chicken broth
- 1 teaspoon lime juice

Method:

1. Season chicken with salt and pepper.
2. Add the coconut oil to a pan over medium heat.
3. Cook onion, garlic and ginger for 5 minutes, stirring often.
4. Add chicken and cook for 10 minutes.
5. Stir in the squash and cook until tender.
6. Pour in milk, broth and lime juice.
7. Reduce heat and simmer for 20 minutes.

Serving Suggestions: Garnish with cilantro.

Preparation & Cooking Tips: This soup can be refrigerated for up to 3 days.

Nutritions Value (Amount per Serving):

- Calories: 325
- Fat: 24.72
- Carbs: 5.75
- Protein: 21.58

Mushroom Soup

Preparation Time: 10 minutes
Cooking Time: 40 minutes
Servings: 5

Ingredients:

- 1 lb. mushrooms
- 28 oz. chicken broth
- ½ teaspoon onion powder
- Pepper to taste
- 1 cup milk

Method:

1. Combine all the ingredients in a pot over medium heat.
2. Bring to a boil.
3. Reduce heat and simmer for 30 minutes.

Serving Suggestions: Garnish with croutons.

Preparation & Cooking Tips: You can also season with garlic powder.

Nutritions Value (Amount per Serving):

- Calories: 267
- Fat: 45
- Carbs: 71.76
- Protein: 45

Beef & Vegetable Soup

Preparation Time: 20 minutes
Cooking Time: 50 minutes
Servings: 4

Ingredients:

- 1 tablespoon olive oil
- 1 onion, chopped
- 1 garlic, chopped
- 1 carrot, chopped
- 1 zucchini, chopped
- Salt and pepper to taste
- 4 cups beef broth
- 1 cup beef, cooked and sliced into strips

Method:

1. Add olive oil to a pot over medium heat.
2. Cook onion and garlic for 3 minutes, stirring often.
3. Add carrot and zucchini.
4. Cook for 10 minutes.
5. Season with salt and pepper.
6. Pour in the beef broth.
7. Add beef strips.
8. Simmer for 40 minutes.

Serving Suggestions: Sprinkle with pepper before serving.

Preparation & Cooking Tips: Use strip steak for this recipe.

Nutritions Value (Amount per Serving):

- Calories: 153
- Fat: 3.75
- Carbs: 28.27
- Protein: 2.66

Broccoli Cream Soup

Preparation Time: 10 minutes
Cooking Time: 20 minutes
Servings: 4

Ingredients:

- 5 cups broccoli florets
- Water
- 1 cup milk
- ½ cup cream
- Salt and pepper to taste

Method:

1. Add broccoli florets to a steamer basket.
2. Pour water into a pot over medium heat.
3. Place steamer basket inside.
4. Steam until tender.
5. Let cool for 15 minutes.
6. Add steamed broccoli to a blender.
7. Process until finely chopped.
8. Transfer to a pot over medium heat.
9. Stir in the rest of the ingredients.
10. Simmer for 10 minutes.

Serving Suggestions: Garnish with croutons.

Nutritions Value (Amount per Serving):

- Calories: 111
- Fat: 8.06
- Carbs: 6.5
- Protein: 4.54

CHAPTER 6: SNACK RECIPES

Vegetable Sandwich with Hummus

Preparation Time: 10 minutes
Cooking Time: 0 minutes
Serving: 1

Ingredients:

- 2 slices whole-wheat bread
- 4 tablespoons hummus
- ¼ avocado, mashed
- ½ cup lettuce, shredded
- ¼ red bell pepper, sliced
- ¼ cup cucumber, sliced
- ¼ cup carrot, shredded

Method:

1. Spread the hummus and mashed avocado on one side of the bread slices.
2. Top with the vegetables.

Serving Suggestions: Serve with your favorite fresh fruit juice.

Preparation & Cooking Tips: This sandwich can be refrigerated for up to 4 hours.

Nutritions Value (Amount per Serving):

- Calories: 206
- Fat: 12.68
- Carbs: 20.72
- Protein: 4.79

Black Bean & Sweet Potato Burger

Preparation Time: 15 minutes
Cooking Time: 30 minutes
Servings: 4

Ingredients:

- ½ cup rolled oats
- ½ cup scallions, chopped
- 1 cup black beans, rinsed and drained
- 2 cups sweet potato, grated
- ¼ cup mayonnaise
- 1 teaspoon curry powder
- 1 tablespoon tomato paste
- Salt to taste
- ¼ cup olive oil
- 4 whole-wheat burger buns
- 1 cup lettuce, shredded

Method:

1. Process rolled oats in the food processor until finely ground.
2. Add to a bowl.
3. Stir in the rest of the ingredients except olive oil, lettuce and buns.
4. Form patties from the mixture.
5. Add oil to a pan over medium heat.
6. Fry the patties until browned on both sides.
7. Serve with buns and lettuce.

Serving Suggestions: Serve with ketchup and mustard.

Preparation & Cooking Tips: Squeeze grated sweet potato to get rid of extra moisture.

Nutritions Value (Amount per Serving):

- Calories: 380
- Fat: 20.02
- Carbs: 42.29
- Protein: 14.5

Roasted Chickpeas

Preparation Time: 10 minutes
Cooking Time: 15 minutes
Servings: 4

Ingredients:

- 15 oz. chickpeas, rinsed and drained
- 1 ½ tablespoons toasted sesame oil
- ¼ teaspoon smoked paprika
- ¼ teaspoon red pepper flakes
- Salt to taste

Method:

1. Combine all the ingredients in a bowl.
2. Spread the mixture in a baking pan.
3. Roast in the oven at 400 degrees F for 10 to 15 minutes or until golden and crispy.

Serving Suggestions: Drizzle with lime juice before serving.

Preparation & Cooking Tips: You can also use olive oil instead of sesame oil.

Nutritions Value (Amount per Serving):

- Calories: 434
- Fat: 9.85
- Carbs: 67.28
- Protein: 21.84

Beet Chips

Preparation Time: 10 minutes
Cooking Time: 3 hours
Servings: 4

Ingredients:

- 2 beets, sliced thinly
- 1 tablespoon olive oil
- Salt to taste

Method:

1. Preheat your oven to 200 degrees F.
2. Drizzle beet slices with olive oil and salt.
3. Spread the beets in a baking pan.
4. Bake in the oven for 3 hours.
5. Let cool for 30 to 40 minutes before serving.

Serving Suggestions: Serve with your dip of choice.

Preparation & Cooking Tips: Store in an airtight jar for up to 3 days.

Nutritions Value (Amount per Serving):

- Calories: 104
- Fat: 3.47
- Carbs: 18.48
- Protein: 0.91

Apple Chips

Preparation Time: 10 minutes
Cooking Time: 3 hours
Servings: 4

Ingredients:

- 4 apples, sliced thinly
- 2 tablespoons olive oil

Method:

1. Preheat your oven to 200 degrees F.
2. Toss apples in olive oil.
3. Bake in the oven for 3 hours.

Serving Suggestions: Serve with unsweetened dip.

Nutritions Value (Amount per Serving):

- Calories: 154
- Fat: 7.06
- Carbs: 25.13
- Protein: 0.47

Sesame Crackers

Preparation Time: 30 minutes
Cooking Time: 20 minutes
Servings: 6

Ingredients:

- 1 ½ cup whole wheat flour
- 4 tablespoons olive oil
- 1 teaspoon salt
- 2 tablespoons flaxseeds, roasted
- 2 tablespoons sesame seeds, roasted
- 4 tablespoons cold water

Method:

1. Combine all the ingredients in a bowl.
2. Knead into a dough.
3. Roll out into a thin layer.
4. Slice to create crackers.
5. Bake in the oven at 350 degrees F for 20 minutes.

Serving Suggestions: Let cool for 15 minutes.

Preparation & Cooking Tips: Store in an airtight container for up to 3 days.

Nutritions Value (Amount per Serving):

- Calories: 217
- Fat: 12.83
- Carbs: 22.9
- Protein: 5.14

Date Bites with Pistachios

Preparation Time: 10 minutes
Cooking Time: 0 minutes
Servings: 32

Ingredients:

- 2 cups whole dates, pitted
- 1 cup pistachios
- 1 cup golden raisins
- 1 teaspoon ground fennel seeds
- Pinch pepper

Method:

1. Add all the ingredients to a food processor.
2. Process until fine.
3. Form balls from the mixture.

Serving Suggestions: Serve immediately or refrigerate for a few minutes first.

Preparation & Cooking Tips: Store in an airtight container for up to 3 hours.

Nutritions Value (Amount per Serving):

- Calories: 64
- Fat: 1.82
- Carbs: 12.22
- Protein: 1.22

Carrot Smoothie

Preparation Time: 10 minutes
Cooking Time: 10 minutes
Servings: 3

Ingredients:

- 1 cup carrots, sliced
- Water
- 1 ½ cups ice cubes
- 1 cup orange juice
- ½ teaspoon orange zest

Method:

1. Boil carrots in water until tender.
2. Drain and transfer to a blender.
3. Stir in the rest of the ingredients.
4. Process until smooth.

Serving Suggestions: Garnish with orange slices.

Nutritions Value (Amount per Serving):

- Calories: 137
- Fat: 5.69
- Carbs: 19.56
- Protein: 1.97

Chai Chia Pudding

Preparation Time: 8 hours and 10 minutes
Cooking Time: 0 minutes
Servings: 2

Ingredients:

- 2 tablespoons chia seeds
- ½ cup almond milk (unsweetened)
- ¼ teaspoon vanilla extract
- 2 teaspoons maple syrup
- ¼ teaspoon ground cinnamon
- Pinch ground cloves
- Pinch ground cardamom
- ½ cup banana, sliced

Method:

1. Combine all the ingredients in a bowl.
2. Cover the bowl.
3. Refrigerate for 8 hours.
4. Top with the banana before serving.

Serving Suggestions: You can also top with roasted pistachios.

Preparation & Cooking Tips: Refrigerate for up to 2 days.

Nutritions Value (Amount per Serving):

- Calories: 139
- Fat: 1.28
- Carbs: 33.13
- Protein: 1.48

Sweet Potato Fries

Preparation Time: 10 minutes
Cooking Time: 15 minutes
Servings: 4

Ingredients:

- 1 tablespoon olive oil
- ¼ teaspoon ground cinnamon
- ¼ teaspoon cayenne pepper
- Salt and pepper to taste
- 2 sweet potatoes, sliced into strips

Method:

1. Mix oil and spices.
2. Toss sweet potato strips in the spice mixture.
3. Spread sweet potato strips in a baking pan.
4. Bake in the oven at 400 degrees F for 15 minutes, stirring once or twice.

Serving Suggestions: Drain and serve immediately.

Preparation & Cooking Tips: Add more cayenne pepper if you like your sweet potato fries spicier.

Nutritions Value (Amount per Serving):

- Calories: 43
- Fat: 3.51
- Carbs: 2.82
- Protein: 0.68

CHAPTER 7: APPETIZER RECIPES

Mushroom Pate

Preparation Time: 15 minutes
Cooking Time: 15 minutes
Servings: 16

Ingredients:

- 1 teaspoon olive oil
- ¼ cup shallots, minced
- 1 lb. mushrooms, chopped
- Salt and pepper to taste
- 2 tablespoons fresh sage, chopped
- 3 tablespoons dry sherry
- 2 tablespoons olive oil
- 2 tablespoons Parmesan cheese
- ½ cup walnuts

Method:

1. Add 1 teaspoon olive oil to a pan over medium heat.
2. Cook shallots for 30 seconds.
3. Stir in mushrooms.
4. Cook for 5 minutes.
5. Season with salt, pepper and sage.
6. Cook for 5 more minutes.
7. Pour in sherry.
8. Cook for 2 minutes.
9. Transfer the mushroom mixture to a blender or food processor.
10. Pour in the remaining oil, walnuts, and Parmesan cheese.
11. Process until finely chopped.

Serving Suggestions: Serve with whole wheat crackers.

Preparation & Cooking Tips: Toast the walnuts first for better flavor.

Nutritions Value (Amount per Serving):

- Calories: 125
- Fat: 4.1
- Carbs: 23.06
- Protein: 3.39

Steamed Zucchini

Preparation Time: 5 minutes
Cooking Time: 10 minutes
Servings: 4

Ingredients:

- Water
- 2 lb. zucchini, sliced thickly

Method:

1. Add water to a pot over medium heat.
2. Bring to a boil.
3. Insert the steamer basket inside the pot.
4. Place the zucchini on top of the steamer basket.
5. Cover the pot.
6. Steam for 5 minutes.

Serving Suggestions: Season with salt and pepper before serving.

Preparation & Cooking Tips: You can also use carrots for this recipe.

Nutritions Value (Amount per Serving):

- Calories: 48
- Fat: 0.91
- Carbs: 7.05
- Protein: 6.15

Garlic Hummus

Preparation Time: 10 minutes
Cooking Time: 0 minutes
Servings: 8

Ingredients:

- 15 oz. chickpeas
- 1 clove garlic, peeled
- ¼ cup olive oil
- ¼ cup lemon juice
- ¼ cup tahini
- ½ teaspoon chili powder
- 1 teaspoon ground cumin
- Pinch salt

Method:

1. Combine all the ingredients in a food processor or blender.
2. Process until pureed.

Serving Suggestions: Serve with pita bread strips.

Nutritions Value (Amount per Serving):

- Calories: 309
- Fat: 14.1
- Carbs: 35.91
- Protein: 12.28

Cucumber Rolls

Preparation Time: 15 minutes
Cooking Time: 0 minutes
Servings: 6

Ingredients:

- 1 avocado, mashed
- 1 teaspoon lemon juice
- Salt and pepper to taste
- 1 cucumber, sliced thinly lengthwise

Method:

1. Mix the mashed avocado, lemon juice, salt and pepper.
2. Top the cucumber with the mixture.
3. Roll up and serve.

Serving Suggestions: Serve immediately.

Preparation & Cooking Tips: Secure with toothpicks.

Nutritions Value (Amount per Serving):

- Calories: 57
- Fat: 4.93
- Carbs: 3.65
- Protein: 0.83

Tomato Salsa

Preparation Time: 15 minutes
Cooking Time: 0 minutes
Servings: 10

Ingredients:

- 4 cups tomatoes, diced
- 1 red onion, minced
- ¼ cup red wine vinegar
- 1 jalapeno, minced
- ½ cup fresh cilantro, chopped
- Salt to taste
- Pinch cayenne pepper

Method:

1. Combine all the ingredients in a bowl.
2. Refrigerate the salsa until ready to serve.

Serving Suggestions: Serve with nacho chips.

Preparation & Cooking Tips: This salsa can be refrigerated for up to 3 days.

Nutritions Value (Amount per Serving):

- Calories: 17
- Fat: 0.14
- Carbs: 3.58
- Protein: 0.69

Avocado Hummus

Preparation Time: 10 minutes
Cooking Time: 0 minutes
Servings: 10

Ingredients:

- 1 avocado, pitted and sliced
- 15 oz. chickpeas
- 1 cup fresh cilantro leaves
- ¼ cup tahini
- ¼ cup olive oil
- ¼ cup lemon juice
- 1 clove garlic, peeled
- 1 teaspoon ground cumin
- Pinch salt

Method:

1. Add all the ingredients to a blender or food processor.
2. Process until pureed.

Serving Suggestions: Serve with pita chips or vegetable dippers.

Nutritions Value (Amount per Serving):

- Calories: 279
- Fat: 14.21
- Carbs: 30.43
- Protein: 10.24

Cheddar Balls

Preparation Time: 10 minutes
Cooking Time: 15 minutes
Servings: 4

Ingredients:

- 2 eggs, beaten
- ½ cup almond flour
- ½ cup cheddar cheese, shredded
- ¼ cup Parmesan cheese, grated
- ¼ cup mozzarella cheese, shredded
- ¼ teaspoon parsley flakes
- ¼ teaspoon garlic powder
- Salt and pepper to taste

Method:

1. Preheat your oven to 400 degrees F.
2. Combine all the ingredients in a bowl.
3. Form balls from the mixture.
4. Bake in the oven for 15 minutes.

Serving Suggestions: Serve with pretzel sticks.

Preparation & Cooking Tips: Store in an airtight container for up to 1 day.

Nutritions Value (Amount per Serving):

- Calories: 207
- Fat: 11.69
- Carbs: 8.94
- Protein: 16.4

Zucchini Chips

Preparation Time: 15 minutes
Cooking Time: 1 hour
Servings: 2

Ingredients:

- 2 zucchini, sliced into rounds
- Cooking spray
- 2 teaspoons lime juice
- ¼ teaspoon chili powder
- Pinch salt

Method:

1. Preheat your oven to 225 degrees F.
2. Spray the zucchini slices with oil.
3. Drizzle with lime juice.
4. Sprinkle with chili powder and salt.
5. Bake zucchini in the oven for 1 hour, flipping twice.

Serving Suggestions: Let cool on a wire rack for 10 minutes before serving.

Preparation & Cooking Tips: Arrange zucchini slices in a single layer in the baking pan.

Nutritions Value (Amount per Serving):

- Calories: 5
- Fat: 0.1
- Carbs: 0.94
- Protein: 0.37

Buffalo Cauliflower

Preparation Time: 15 minutes
Cooking Time: 30 minutes
Servings: 6

Ingredients:

- 4 cups cauliflower florets
- 2 tablespoons olive oil
- 1 tablespoon lemon juice
- 1/3 cup hot sauce
- 3 tablespoons butter
- 1 tablespoon tomato paste
- Salt and pepper to taste

Method:

1. Preheat your oven to 400 degrees F.
2. Toss the cauliflower in the olive oil.
3. Bake in the oven for 30 minutes.
4. Mix the remaining ingredients in a bowl.
5. Stir cauliflower into the sauce and serve.

Serving Suggestions: Garnish with scallions.

Nutritions Value (Amount per Serving):

- Calories: 116
- Fat: 10.54
- Carbs: 5.16
- Protein: 1.77

Vegetable Relish

Preparation Time: 30 minutes
Cooking Time: 0 minutes
Servings: 6

Ingredients:

Vegetables
- 1 red onion, minced
- 1 tomato, chopped
- 1 red bell pepper, chopped
- 1 yellow bell pepper, chopped
- 1 green bell pepper, chopped
- ½ cucumber, chopped
- 2 zucchini, chopped

Dressing
- 1 clove garlic, minced
- 1 teaspoon dried oregano
- ½ cup olive oil
- 3 tablespoons red wine vinegar
- Salt and pepper to taste

Method:

1. Mix vegetable ingredients in a bowl.
2. In another bowl, combine dressing ingredients.
3. Pour dressing into the vegetable relish.
4. Stir well.
5. Serve immediately or refrigerate until ready to serve.

Serving Suggestions: Top with crumbled feta cheese before serving.

Preparation & Cooking Tips: Use red wine vinegar for the dressing.

Nutritions Value (Amount per Serving):

- Calories: 188
- Fat: 18.17
- Carbs: 6.12
- Protein: 1.23

CHAPTER 8: SIDE DISH RECIPES

Cucumber Salad

Preparation Time: 15 minutes
Cooking Time: 0 minutes
Servings: 4

Ingredients:

- 2 cucumbers, sliced thinly lengthwise
- ¼ cup rice vinegar
- 1 teaspoon sugar
- Pinch salt
- 2 tablespoons sesame seeds

Method:

1. Combine all the ingredients in a bowl.
2. Stir well.

Serving Suggestions: Serve immediately or refrigerate for 15 minutes before serving.

Preparation & Cooking Tips: Toast sesame seeds first for better dish flavor.

Nutritions Value (Amount per Serving):

- Calories: 31
- Fat: 2.45
- Carbs: 1.31
- Protein: 0.84

Sautéed Squash

Preparation Time: 15 minutes
Cooking Time: 15 minutes
Servings: 7

Ingredients:

- 1 butternut squash, sliced into cubes
- 1 tablespoon olive oil

Method:

1. Pour the oil into a pan over medium heat.
2. Cook squash for 15 minutes, stirring frequently.

Serving Suggestions: Sprinkle with dried herbs.

Preparation & Cooking Tips: This dish can be made ahead. Peel and slice into cubes. Cover and refrigerate for up to 3 days.

Nutritions Value (Amount per Serving):

- Calories: 26
- Fat: 1.95
- Carbs: 2.34
- Protein: 0.2

Sautéed Mushroom & Zucchini

Preparation Time: 15 minutes
Cooking Time: 15 minutes
Servings: 4

Ingredients:

- 2 teaspoons olive oil
- 2 zucchini, sliced into rounds
- 1½ cups mushrooms, sliced
- 2 teaspoons fresh basil, chopped
- Salt and pepper to taste

Method:

1. Pour oil into a pan over medium high heat.
2. Cook zucchini for 2 to 3 minutes, stirring often.
3. Stir in the mushrooms.
4. Season with basil, salt and pepper.
5. Cook while stirring for 1 minute.

Serving Suggestions: Serve with grilled main course.

Preparation & Cooking Tips: Dried basil can also be used if fresh basil is not available.

Nutritions Value (Amount per Serving):

- Calories: 27
- Fat: 2.31
- Carbs: 1.45
- Protein: 0.5

Vegetable Sauté

Preparation Time: 15 minutes
Cooking Time: 7 minutes
Servings: 4

Ingredients:

- 1 tablespoon olive oil
- 1 shallot, minced
- 4 cups mixed frozen vegetables
- ½ teaspoon dried dill
- Salt and pepper to taste

Method:

1. Pour oil into a pan over medium heat.
2. Cook shallot for 1 minute.
3. Add vegetables.
4. Cover the pan.
5. Cook for 6 minutes, stirring often.
6. Season with dill, salt and pepper.

Serving Suggestions: Garnish with lemon wedges.

Preparation & Cooking Tips: Tarragon can also be used in place of dill.

Nutritions Value (Amount per Serving):

- Calories: 153
- Fat: 3.71
- Carbs: 25.04
- Protein: 5.47

Tarragon Asparagus

Preparation Time: 20 minutes
Cooking Time: 20 minutes
Servings: 4

Ingredients:

Asparagus
- 4 cups asparagus, trimmed

Dressing
- 4 teaspoons olive oil
- 2 teaspoons balsamic vinegar
- Pinch salt
- 1 clove garlic, crushed
- 2 teaspoons fresh tarragon

Method:

1. Preheat your oven to 400 degrees F.
2. Combine the dressing ingredients in a bowl.
3. Stir well.
4. Add asparagus to the bowl.
5. Coat evenly with dressing.
6. Spread asparagus on a baking pan.
7. Bake in the oven for 20 minutes, flipping once or twice.

Serving Suggestions: Sprinkle with Parmesan cheese before serving.

Preparation & Cooking Tips: If fresh tarragon is not available, use dried instead.

Nutritions Value (Amount per Serving):

- Calories: 71
- Fat: 4.69
- Carbs: 6.05
- Protein: 3.08

Pickled Beets

Preparation Time: 45 minutes
Cooking Time: 10 minutes
Servings: 4

Ingredients:

- ½ cup red wine vinegar
- 1 red onion, sliced thinly
- 2 tablespoons sugar
- 2 whole cloves
- 4 whole peppercorns
- 1 cinnamon stick
- 3 cups beets, sliced into cubes and steamed

Method:

1. Pour the vinegar into a pot over medium heat.
2. Stir in the rest of the ingredients except the beets.
3. Bring to a boil.
4. Reduce heat and simmer for 5 minutes.
5. Turn off heat.
6. Transfer mixture to a bowl.
7. Add the beets and stir to coat evenly.
8. Marinate for 30 minutes.

Serving Suggestions: Serve with grilled entrée.

Preparation & Cooking Tips: Beets can also be sliced into wedges or strips depending on your preference.

Nutritions Value (Amount per Serving):

- Calories: 151
- Fat: 0.26
- Carbs: 37.77
- Protein: 1.71

Cucumber & Carrot Salad

Preparation Time: 2 hours and 15 minutes
Cooking Time: 0 minutes
Servings: 4

Ingredients:

- ¼ cup rice wine vinegar
- 1 tablespoon toasted sesame oil
- ⅛ teaspoon chipotle chili powder
- 2 tablespoons fresh cilantro, chopped
- Salt and pepper to taste
- ½ cup onion, sliced thinly
- 2 carrots, sliced into thin strips
- 1 cucumber, sliced into rounds

Method:

1. In a bowl, mix the rice wine vinegar, sesame oil, chili powder, cilantro, salt and pepper.
2. Mix well.
3. Add the onion, carrots and cucumber.
4. Coat evenly with sauce.
5. Cover and refrigerate for 2 hours before serving.

Serving Suggestions: Serve with fish entrée.

Preparation & Cooking Tips: The salad can be refrigerated for up to 4 hours.

Nutritions Value (Amount per Serving):

- Calories: 45
- Fat: 3.46
- Carbs: 2.8
- Protein: 0.43

Moroccan Mashed Potatoes

Preparation Time: 15 minutes
Cooking Time: 30 minutes
Servings: 32

Ingredients:

- 10 potatoes, peeled and sliced into cubes
- Water
- 3 tablespoons olive oil, divided
- 1 onion, minced
- 1 tablespoon ground turmeric
- ½ teaspoon ground cumin
- Salt and pepper to taste

Method:

1. Add the potatoes to a pot over medium heat.
2. Cover with water.
3. Cook until tender.
4. Drain and transfer to a plate.
5. Mash with a fork until creamy.
6. Pour 1 tablespoon olive oil into a pan over medium heat.
7. Cook onion for 5 minutes, stirring often.
8. Add onion to the mashed potatoes.
9. Stir in the rest of the ingredients and remaining olive oil.
10. Mix until fully combined.

Serving Suggestions: Sprinkle with a little pepper on top before serving.

Preparation & Cooking Tips: You can add a tablespoon of milk to the mashed potatoes to make it creamier.

Nutritions Value (Amount per Serving):

- Calories: 103
- Fat: 1.39
- Carbs: 20.81
- Protein: 2.43

Cucumber Kimchi

Preparation Time: 12 hours and 45 minutes
Cooking Time: 0 minutes
Servings: 6

Ingredients:

- 2 cucumbers, sliced into half moons
- 1 teaspoon salt
- 2 scallions, chopped
- 2 cloves garlic, minced
- 1 tablespoon ginger, grated
- 2 tablespoons rice vinegar
- ½ teaspoon fish sauce
- 2 teaspoons sugar
- 1 tablespoon Korean chili powder

Method:

1. Toss cucumber slices in salt.
2. Let sit at room temperature for 30 minutes.
3. In a bowl, mix the remaining ingredients.
4. Rinse and drain the cucumbers.
5. Add the cucumbers to the mixture.
6. Cover the bowl.
7. Refrigerate for 12 hours before serving.

Serving Suggestions: Stir before serving.

Preparation & Cooking Tips: This can be refrigerated for up to 1 week.

Nutritions Value (Amount per Serving):

- Calories: 12
- Fat: 0.22
- Carbs: 2.48
- Protein: 0.39

Sautéed Onion & Peppers

Preparation Time: 20 minutes
Cooking Time: 20 minutes
Servings: 12

Ingredients:

- 2 tablespoons olive oil
- 1 onion, sliced thinly
- 1 red bell pepper, sliced thinly
- 1 yellow bell pepper, sliced thinly
- 1 orange bell pepper, sliced thinly
- 1 green bell pepper, sliced thinly
- Salt and pepper to taste

Method:

1. Pour oil into a pan over medium heat.
2. Cook onion and bell peppers for 20 minutes, stirring often.
3. Season with salt and pepper.

Serving Suggestions: Serve with chicken dish.

Preparation & Cooking Tips: Use white or yellow onion for this recipe.

Nutritions Value (Amount per Serving):

- Calories: 28
- Fat: 2.29
- Carbs: 1.84
- Protein: 0.38

CHAPTER 9: DESSERT RECIPES

Peanut Butter Balls

Preparation Time: 30 minutes
Cooking Time: 0 minutes
Servings: 12

Ingredients:

- ½ cup peanut butter
- ¾ cup crispy rice cereal
- 1 teaspoon maple syrup

Method:

1. Combine all the ingredients in a bowl.
2. Form balls from the mixture.
3. Place the balls in a baking pan lined with parchment.
4. Freeze for 15 minutes.

Serving Suggestions: Coat the balls with melted dark chocolate before serving.

Preparation & Cooking Tips: Almond butter can also be used in place of peanut butter.

Nutritions Value (Amount per Serving):

- Calories: 39
- Fat: 1.94
- Carbs: 4.44
- Protein: 0.86

Apple Bars

Preparation Time: 20 minutes
Cooking Time: 30 minutes
Servings: 16

Ingredients:

- Cooking spray

Dry ingredients

- 1 ½ cups all purpose flour
- ¾ teaspoon baking powder
- 1 cup brown sugar
- 1 cup rolled oats
- 1 teaspoon lemon zest
- ¼ teaspoon ground nutmeg
- ½ teaspoon ground cinnamon
- ½ teaspoon salt

Wet ingredients

- 3 tablespoons canola oil
- 2 apples, peeled and sliced thinly
- ¼ cup apple juice concentrate
- ¼ cup walnuts, chopped

Method:

1. Preheat your oven to 350 degrees F.
2. Spray your baking pan with oil.
3. In a bowl, mix the dry ingredients.
4. In another bowl, combine the wet ingredients.
5. Add dry mixture to the wet mixture.
6. Mix well.
7. Pour mixture into the baking pan.
8. Bake in the oven for 30 minutes.

Serving Suggestions: Let cool on a wire rack for 15 minutes before serving.

Preparation & Cooking Tips: Use tart apples for this recipe.

Nutritions Value (Amount per Serving):

- Calories: 141
- Fat: 3.99
- Carbs: 27.3
- Protein: 2.1

Mango & Pineapple Ice Cream

Preparation Time: 10 minutes
Cooking Time: 0 minutes
Servings: 6

Ingredients:

- 16 oz. canned pineapple chunks
- 1 cup mango, peeled and chopped
- 1 tablespoon lime juice
- ¼ cup water

Method:

1. Add all the ingredients to a blender or food processor.
2. Process until pureed.
3. Freeze until firm or process using an ice cream machine.

Serving Suggestions: Garnish with pineapple slice.

Preparation & Cooking Tips: Use freshly squeezed lime juice.

Nutritions Value (Amount per Serving):

- Calories: 82
- Fat: 0.18
- Carbs: 21.11
- Protein: 0.54

Strawberry Ice Cream

Preparation Time: 10 minutes
Cooking Time: 0 minutes
Servings: 4

Ingredients:

- 1 lb. fresh strawberries, sliced
- 2 bananas, sliced
- 1 tablespoon lemon juice
- ¼ cup ice-cold water, as needed

Method:

1. Add all the ingredients to a blender or food processor.
2. Pulse until smooth.
3. Freeze until firm.

Serving Suggestions: Serve with wafers.

Preparation & Cooking Tips: Use freshly squeezed lemon juice.

Nutritions Value (Amount per Serving):

- Calories: 210
- Fat: 1.25
- Carbs: 53.11
- Protein: 2.72

Grilled Pineapple

Preparation Time: 10 minutes
Cooking Time: 6 minutes
Servings: 6

Ingredients:

- 1 tablespoon olive oil
- 1 tablespoon lime juice
- 3 tablespoons brown sugar
- 1 ½ teaspoons chili powder
- 1 tablespoon agave nectar
- Pinch salt
- 6 pineapple slices or rings

Method:

1. In a bowl, combine all the ingredients except pineapple.
2. Brush pineapple with the mixture.
3. Grill pineapple slices for 3 minutes per side.

Preparation & Cooking Tips: Honey can also be used in place of agave nectar.

Nutritions Value (Amount per Serving):

- Calories: 60
- Fat: 2.39
- Carbs: 10.27
- Protein: 0.33

Marinated Oranges

Preparation Time: 3 hours and 15 minutes
Cooking Time: 0 minutes
Servings: 4

Ingredients:

- 1 cup orange juice
- 1 tablespoon orange zest
- 1 tablespoon lemon juice
- 1 teaspoon lemon zest
- 1 tablespoon sugar
- 1 teaspoon vanilla extract
- 3 cups oranges, peeled and sliced

Method:

1. Add all the ingredients except oranges to a bowl.
2. Stir until the sugar has been dissolved.
3. Add the oranges to the mixture.
4. Cover and refrigerate for 3 hours.

Serving Suggestions: Serve with plain Greek yogurt.

Preparation & Cooking Tips: You can also use lime or lemon zest for garnishing.

Nutritions Value (Amount per Serving):

- Calories: 136
- Fat: 0.32
- Carbs: 31.66
- Protein: 1.74

Berries with Custard

Preparation Time: 50 minutes
Cooking Time: 15 minutes
Servings: 4

Ingredients:

- 2 egg yolks
- 1 cup half and half cream
- 2 tablespoons sugar
- 2 teaspoons vanilla extract
- ½ cup raspberries
- ½ cup strawberries
- ½ cup blueberries
- ½ cup blackberries

Method:

1. Add the egg yolks, cream and sugar to a pan over low heat.
2. Cook while stirring until thickened.
3. Transfer mixture to a bowl.
4. Stir in the vanilla.
5. Cover and refrigerate for 30 minutes.
6. Stir in the berries and serve.

Serving Suggestions: Garnish with fresh herb sprigs.

Nutritions Value (Amount per Serving):

- Calories: 176
- Fat: 3.31
- Carbs: 33.09
- Protein: 3.87

Carrot Cake Balls

Preparation Time: 30 minutes
Cooking Time: 0 minutes
Servings: 24

Ingredients:

- ½ cup rolled oats
- 1 cup dates, pitted and sliced
- ¼ cup chia seeds
- ¼ cup pecans, chopped
- 2 carrots, grated
- ¼ teaspoon ground turmeric
- ½ teaspoon ground ginger
- ¾ teaspoon ground cinnamon
- 1 teaspoon vanilla extract
- Pinch salt

Method:

1. Add oats, dates, chia seeds and pecans to a blender or food processor.
2. Pulse until fine.
3. Stir in the rest of the ingredients.
4. Form balls from the mixture.

Preparation & Cooking Tips: These can be frozen for up to 3 months.

Nutritions Value (Amount per Serving):

- Calories: 55
- Fat: 2.37
- Carbs: 8.65
- Protein: 1.42

Oat & Peanut Butter Balls

Preparation Time: 45 minutes
Cooking Time: 0 minutes
Servings: 12

Ingredients:

- ¾ cup dates, pitted and chopped
- Hot water
- ½ cup rolled oats
- ¼ cup peanut butter

Method:

1. Soak the dates in hot water for 15 minutes.
2. Drain and transfer to a blender or food processor.
3. Add peanut butter and rolled oats.
4. Process until fine.
5. Transfer mixture to a bowl.
6. Form balls from the mixture.
7. Refrigerate for 15 minutes.

Serving Suggestions: Serve with chia seeds.

Preparation & Cooking Tips: Use creamy natural peanut butter for this recipe.

Nutritions Value (Amount per Serving):

- Calories: 51
- Fat: 1.27
- Carbs: 10.81
- Protein: 1.27

Purple Fruit Salad

Preparation Time: 15 minutes
Cooking Time: 0 minutes
Servings: 8

Ingredients:

- 2 cups blueberries, sliced in half
- 2 cups grapes, sliced in half
- 2 plums, peeled and diced
- 1 tablespoon fresh basil, chopped

Method:

1. Combine the fruits in a bowl.
2. Top with the fresh basil.

Serving Suggestions: Serve with lime yogurt salad dressing.

Preparation & Cooking Tips: You can also refrigerate for 30 minutes before serving.

Nutritions Value (Amount per Serving):

- Calories: 93
- Fat: 0.29
- Carbs: 23.63
- Protein: 0.74

CHAPTER 10: 21-DAY MEAL PLAN

Day 1

Breakfast: Breakfast Bowl

Lunch: Chickpea Curry

Dinner: Roasted Root Vegetables

Day 2

Breakfast: Berry Breakfast Smoothie

Lunch: Potato Curry

Dinner: Vegan Buddha Bowl

Day 3

Breakfast: Cinnamon Oats

Lunch: Tofu Stir Fry

Dinner: Lemon Roasted Cauliflower & Broccoli

Day 4

Breakfast: Oatmeal with Chia & Quinoa

Lunch: Mushroom & Barley Risotto

Dinner: Black Bean Salad

Day 5

Breakfast: Blueberry & Almond Pudding

Lunch: Roasted Tofu

Dinner: Chickpea & Avocado Salad

Day 6

Breakfast: Breakfast Bowl

Lunch: Chickpea Curry

Dinner: Sautéed Cauliflower

Day 7

Breakfast: Oatmeal with Chia & Quinoa

Lunch: Potatoes with Beans & Salsa

Dinner: Chickpea & Avocado Salad

Day 8

Breakfast: Blueberry & Almond Pudding

Lunch: Tuna Salad

Dinner: Roasted Tofu

Day 9

Breakfast: Breakfast Bowl

Lunch: Lemon Roasted Cauliflower & Broccoli

Dinner: Black Bean Salad

Day 10

Breakfast: Berry Breakfast Smoothie

Lunch: Vegan Buddha Bowl

Dinner: Garlic Squash

Day 11

Breakfast: Avocado Toast with Tuna

Lunch: Superfood Salad

Dinner: Butternut Squash Carbonara

Day 12

Breakfast: Blueberry & Almond Pudding

Lunch: Sesame Beets

Dinner: Mushroom & Barley Risotto

Day 13

Breakfast: Berry, Almond & Coconut Smoothie Bowl

Lunch: Roasted Tofu

Dinner: Potato Curry

Day 14

Breakfast: Breakfast Bowl

Lunch: Kale, Sweet Potato & Tofu Salad

Dinner: Sautéed Cauliflower

Day 15

Breakfast: Peanut Butter Toast with Banana

Lunch: Chickpea Curry

Dinner: Black Bean Salad

Day 16

Breakfast: Oatmeal

Lunch: Orange & Arugula Salad

Dinner: Sesame Beets

Day 17

Breakfast: Blueberry Cereal

Lunch: Beef & Butternut Squash Stew

Dinner: Tuna Salad

Day 18

Breakfast: Avocado Toast with Tuna

Lunch: Butternut Squash Carbonara

Dinner: Garlic Squash

Day 19

Breakfast: Oatmeal

Lunch: Vegan Buddha Bowl

Dinner: Superfood Salad

Day 20

Breakfast: Blueberry Cereal

Lunch: Orange & Arugula Salad

Dinner: Kale, Sweet Potato & Tofu Salad

Day 21

Breakfast: Peanut Butter Toast with Banana

Lunch: Sautéed Cauliflower

Dinner: Beef & Butternut Squash Stew

CONCLUSION

Diabetes is a disease that you can live with and manage properly.

Just make sure that you follow a proper diet that will help you maintain proper levels of blood sugar.

With the recipes that you have in this book, you can still enjoy your favorite dishes without putting your health at risk.

And because almost all these are easy to prepare and ready in no time, you can make these dishes even during the busiest of days.

Enjoy!

happy cooking

APPENDIX RECIPE INDEX

Made in the USA
Columbia, SC
29 September 2023

23621164R00063